KEEPING PETS

Dogs

Louise and Richard Spilsbury

Heinemann Library
Chicago, Illinois

Design by Richard Parker and Q2A Solutions
Printed and bound in China by
South China Printing Company

10 09 08 07 06
10 9 8 7 6 5 4 3 2 1

Library of Congress Cataloging-in-Publication Data
Spilsbury, Louise.
   Dogs / Louise and Richard Spilsbury.
      p. cm. -- (Keeping pets)
   Includes bibliographical references and index.
   ISBN 1-4034-7699-3 (library binding-hardcover)
   1. Dogs--Juvenile literature. I. Spilsbury, Richard, 1963- II. Title. III. Series.
   SF426.5S6625 2006
   636.7--dc22
                           2005026292

Acknowledgments
The author and publishers are grateful to the following for permission to reproduce copyright material:
Alamy Images pp. **5 t** (Bob Jackson), **8 b** (Brent Ward), **12 r** (Dave Porter), **12 l** (Esa Hiltula), **8 t** (Imagebroker), **title m**, **9 t** (Juniors Bildarchiv), **43** (Sylvia Cordaly Photo Library Ltd/Corbis); Ardea p. **38** (John Daniels); Art Directors and Trip p. **7 m**; Corbis pp. **11 m**, **21 b**, **45 b**; Corbis pp. **24 b** (Ariel Skelley), **35 t** (Philip James Corwin), **40** (Raymond Gehman); Eye Ubiquitous p. **33** (Hutchison); Getty Images pp. **9 b** (National Geographic/Bill Curtsinger), **4** (The Image Bank); Getty Images (PhotoDisc) pp. **title r**, **5 m**, **23**, **45 l**; Getty Images (Taxi) pp. **15**, **18 m**, **19**, **35 inset**; Harcourt Education Ltd (Tudor Photography) pp. **title left**, **6**, **11 t**, **11 b**, **14**, **16**, **18 b**, **20 t**, **20 b**, **21 t**, **22**, **23 t**, **23 b**, **24 t**, **25**, **26 t**, **26 b**, **27**, **28**, **29 t**, **29 b**, **30**, **31**, **32 t**, **32 b**, **34**, **36 t**, **36 b**, **39 t**, **39 b**, **42**, **45 r**; Superstock (Age Fotostock) pp. **7 top**, **13**; The Kennel Club Photograph Library p. **17**; Virginia Stroud-Lewis p. **41**.

Cover photograph reproduced with permission of Digital Vision.

Every effort has been made to contact copyright holders of any material reproduced in this book. Any omissions will be rectified in subsequent printings if notice is given to the publishers.

The paper used to print this book comes from sustainable resources.

Contents

Any words appearing in the text in bold, **like this**, are explained in the Glossary.

What Is a Dog?

Dogs are among the most popular pets in the world. Dog lovers say dogs make the best pets because they are very friendly, intelligent, faithful, and a lot of fun. Pet dogs usually become an important and much loved part of a family.

Golden retrievers are one of the most popular types of dog. Larger dogs like this make great pets if you like being outdoors and walking.

Domestication

Pet dogs are **descendants** of wild wolves. Around 12,000 years ago, wild wolves came to villages looking for food. People began to use them to help hunt wild animals for food and to defend their farm animals against **predators** such as bears. Gradually dogs began to live side by side with humans. Dogs became the first animals to be **domesticated**.

Breeds

Over time, people bred different types of dog, called **breeds**. People selected animals with certain features and abilities. For example, some types of dog with good **senses** of sight or smell were bred to hunt animals.

Some small dogs were bred to be pets. By the 19th century, pet dogs were so popular that dog clubs, called **kennel clubs**, were formed.

Dogs come in all shapes and sizes, so there is a dog for almost everyone.

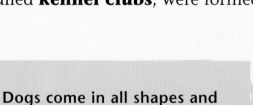

Dogs can make very affectionate, loyal, and devoted pets.

The earliest pet dog?

The earliest evidence we have of people keeping dogs as pets is from 12,000 years ago. The skeleton of a man holding a puppy was found in the country that is now Israel.

Need to know

In most countries, there are laws to protect dogs. These say that people must provide their dog with exercise, care, food, and water. People must never treat dogs badly. By law, dogs must have a **license**, which should be attached to the dog's collar. You should register your dog with a veterinarian.

Dog Facts

Dogs are **mammals**. Mammals are warm-blooded. That means they can warm up or cool down to keep their body at a steady temperature. Mammals give birth to live babies. They also **suckle** their young on milk from their own body.

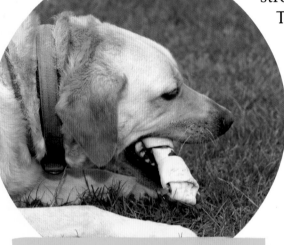

All dogs have certain features in common. They are carnivores (meat-eaters) and have strong teeth for biting through bone. They walk on their toes rather than on the soles (bottom) of their feet. Dogs also pant to help them cool down when they are hot.

Dogs have sharp chewing teeth and sharp **incisors** at the front of the mouth.

Did you know?

- Dogs live for between eight and fifteen years.
- Male dogs are called dogs.
- Female dogs are called bitches.
- Baby dogs are called puppies.

Puppies

A female dog can have up to twelve puppies in one **litter** and can have two litters a year. Puppies are born with their eyes shut and their ears tightly folded and closed. They suckle from their mother every few hours and grow quickly. Puppies need to stay with their mother until they are about eight weeks old. Puppies become adult dogs when they are about one year old, depending on what **breed** they are.

Pack animals

Wild dogs, such as wolves, live in groups called packs. A pet dog thinks of the people in its home as members of its pack. That is why dogs are friendly and faithful and like to do things with you. It also means that dogs become very unhappy if they are left on their own for long periods of time.

Puppies are born helpless. They can only smell, taste, and feel things.

Dogs are pack animals. They like to be with other dogs or people.

Dog senses

A dog's best **senses** are smell and hearing. A dog can hear sounds from much farther away than we can, and its sense of smell is 40 times better than a human's. That is why the police use dogs to sniff out evidence.

7

Types of dog

There are many types, or **breeds**, of dog. They differ greatly in size. They also differ in shape, hair type, and color.

The smaller breeds

The smallest breeds include the toy dogs, such as the King Charles spaniel, toy poodle, and the chihuahua. Most toy dogs weigh less than 11 pounds (5 kilograms). They were bred to be small, so they could be held easily and be good companions. Other small dog breeds include many terriers and the dachshund. The dachshund has short legs and a long body. It is sometimes called a weiner dog because of its shape!

Poodles have curly hair.

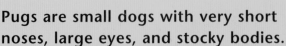
Did you know?
The name *terrier* comes from the Latin word for "earth." Terriers were bred to go down tunnels. The terrier would force out wild animals, such as rabbits. People could then catch the animals for food.

Pugs are small dogs with very short noses, large eyes, and stocky bodies.

The larger breeds

Some of the largest breeds of dog were originally bred to guard or rescue people. These include Rottweilers, Dobermans, St. Bernards, and Great Danes. The heaviest dog breed is the mastiff, which can be as heavy as an adult man.

The tallest breed of dog is the Irish wolfhound. Adult Irish wolfhounds may stand 4.3 feet (1.3 meters) high at the shoulder. The Irish wolfhound and some other large hounds, including the greyhound and Afghan, hunt animals by sight. Basset hounds and bloodhounds hunt using their excellent **sense** of smell. Both have big noses, long ears, and red, bloodshot eyes.

The Irish setter is a medium to large dog with long, wavy red-brown hair.

Mixed breeds

Most people do not have **pedigree** (purebred) dogs as pets. They have mixed-breed dogs. These are also called mongrels. They are **descendants** of different breeds. Their appearance and personality are usually a mix of what their parents and grandparents are like. Mixed-breed dogs are common. They are usually cheaper to buy and are sometimes easier to care for than purebred dogs.

Pedigree dogs

Some people prefer to keep pedigree dogs. These are purebred animals with known parents and grandparents of the same breed. Their history is recorded and registered with a national **kennel club**. These animals are expensive to buy.

Mixed-breed dogs are often healthier than purebreds.

Is a Dog for You?

Dogs can make excellent pets for many people, but they are not right for everyone. Having a dog is a big commitment, and so the whole family needs to think very carefully about whether or not to get a pet dog. Here are some of the points you need to consider before you make a decision.

Dog good points

- Dogs make good companions because they like to be with people or other animals.
- They are active and awake when you are.
- They are all individuals and have their own personality, just like people.
- Many dogs can live up to fifteen years (so you can enjoy their company for a long time).

Dog not-so-good points

- Dogs can be expensive pets. They eat a lot and need to be taken to the veterinarian regularly.
- You have to clean up after them on walks when they go to the bathroom.
- Dogs take up a lot of your time. You have to train them and also give them attention and exercise every day.
- Most dogs need a lot of space.
- Some dogs, especially puppies, may chew, scratch, and ruin things, especially if left alone.

Yes or no?

So, are dogs for you? Do you really have the time, space, money, and energy it takes to have a pet dog? Do you and your family have time to walk, play with, feed, and cuddle a dog every day? Can you find someone to take care of your dog when you are away? If you are prepared to do all these things, even when you are tired or have a lot of homework, then perhaps you are ready to have a pet dog.

A dog will need your attention, time, and interest for all of its life.

Some dogs are very lively. You will need a lot of energy to keep up with them.

Top tip

If you cannot have a dog of your own, there are other ways to enjoy these animals. You could help out at an **animal shelter** or you could help friends or neighbors walk their dogs.

If dogs are left alone too long, they get bored. If this happens, they may chew on furniture, bark, or make a mess.

Choosing Your Dog

One of the things to consider when choosing a dog is its **breed**. There are some general things to consider about different breeds. For example, long-haired dogs need more **grooming** (brushing). Larger breeds usually need more space to live in, more food, and often more exercise than smaller breeds. Some breeds, such as collies and springer spaniels, need to be constantly busy. Otherwise, they get very bored and can behave badly or be destructive. Yet they are also very intelligent, so they are really fun to train.

The right breed

The chart opposite lists a few of the most popular dog breeds and their typical personality. It is more difficult to predict the personality of a mixed-breed dog. When you choose any breed of dog, find out as much as you can about it from books, veterinarians, pet stores, and dog owners. Then, you will know if it is the right breed for you. You can find out more about the different breeds by looking at one of the books listed on page 47.

Bichon frises are happy and curious dogs. They need lots of grooming to keep their hair looking good.

The Doberman is usually calmer and steadier than collies, setters, and spaniels. It also barks less.

Breed	Personalities
Labrador retriever	Intelligent and even-tempered. Good with children. Needs space and exercise. Loves to get in water.
German shepherd	Loyal to owner and suspicious of strangers. Not always good with children. Needs careful training to behave well and not to bite.
Staffordshire bull terrier	Very strong and sometimes difficult to control, so it needs careful training. Gets enough exercise from some short and some long walks.
Border collie	Needs a lot of exercise and activity so that it does not get bored. May get upset or scared by loud noises.
Whippet	Quiet, gentle, and loyal. Very fast runner. Needs to be kept on a secure leash outside to stop it from chasing other animals.
Pomeranian	Good companion that does not need too much space. Can bark a lot.
Poodle	Bright, lively, and easy to train because it is eager to please. Usually devoted to its family; some may bark a lot.
Dalmatian	Full of energy. Can be a bit of a handful and needs a lot of exercise.
Spaniel	Playful and likes being with people. Intelligent and good with children.

Border collies were bred to round up sheep on hills. They are nearly impossible to tire out!

Male or female?

Both male and female dogs make good pets. Female dogs demand more attention, are friendlier, and are often easier to train. Male dogs tend to be more independent. They are usually calmer than females. Sometimes they can be more difficult to train and control. Some male dogs may fight or try to chase other animals.

What age?

Many people like the idea of getting a puppy, but for the first few months a puppy needs someone at home all or most of the day. She needs several meals a day and needs to be let out to go to the bathroom frequently, day and night. A puppy also needs training and may chew and damage things while its teeth are developing. Most puppies should not leave their mothers until they are about eight weeks old.

There are a lot of advantages to getting an older dog. Since older dogs are usually **house-trained**, they do not make a mess. They are usually already used to people. They are probably well behaved and make good companions.

Both male and female dogs make great pets.

Neutering

Every year, thousands of puppies are abandoned because people cannot find homes for them. Females should be **spayed** and male dogs **neutered** by six months old so they cannot have babies. Neutering also makes dogs gentler, friendlier, less likely to run off, and easier to live with.

One or more?

It is fine to get one dog. A dog will be happy with your company. Dogs do not need other dogs around. In fact, some **breeds** of dog, such as terriers, are better alone than with other dogs because they may fight each other. If you decide to have more than one dog, remember that this means more time, money, and effort.

Top tip

When you choose a name for your pet dog, make sure it is a name you like. You will be calling it out a lot when it is time for a walk or for dinner.

Two dogs of different breeds can live happily together.

Where to get your dog

You can get a dog from different types of places. Many people get a dog from an **animal shelter**. These are places that take in abandoned or badly treated dogs. Getting a dog from an animal shelter has good and bad points. People at the animal shelter will advise you on exactly what type of dog is right for you. The dogs will have seen a veterinarian and will have had all the **vaccinations** they need. Most of the dogs are happy, healthy, and ready for a new home. But some dogs end up at a shelter because they have been badly treated. They can be nervous and need extra love and attention. When you take a dog home from an animal shelter, you are giving it a second chance for a happy life.

You can buy puppies from a **breeder**. This is better than buying puppies from a pet shop because breeders can give you all the details about a puppy's parents, its date of birth, and background. You should always be able to meet the puppy's parents to see what it will be like when it grows up.

A dog from a shelter can make a very loyal and loving pet.

Making careful choices

Wherever you go to choose your dog, make sure it is a place that is clean and comfortable for the animals. Take an adult with you and look at several dogs before you make your final choice together. Do not rush into a decision: take time to watch the dogs. Visit several times so you can get to know the personality of the dog you like. Ask to hold or stroke the dog, and see how it gets along with people and if it is used to being handled.

Remember that cute puppies often grow into big dogs. Dalmatian puppies are cute, but adult Dalmatians are a handful for many dog owners.

Top tips

When choosing a dog, here are some things to look out for.

- Do not choose a puppy or dog that has runny eyes, matted fur, or a dirty bottom.
- If one puppy in a **litter** is sick, others may get sick, too.
- Always ask to see the mother of a puppy you choose, to see what she is like.
- Look for an animal that is lively and playful. It should not attack or bite the other puppies around it.

What Do I Need?

Before bringing your puppy or dog home, you need to have everything ready. You will need a place for the dog to sleep, such as a kennel or a crate. You will also need a collar and a leash, bowls for food and water, and toys.

Dog bed

Dogs sleep around fourteen hours a day. They need a comfortable place to rest that is quiet, and where they will not get too hot or too cold. You can make a dog bed out of a wooden box with a blanket and pillow inside. Or, you can buy a dog bed, a dog basket, or a beanbag.

Some people buy a crate. A crate is like a large cage, which is big enough for the dog to stand, stretch, and turn around in. You need to put easily washable old towels or blankets inside to make the crate comfortable to sleep in. To a dog, a crate is a kind of cave, and most dogs like being in them because they feel safe there.

You should wash your dog's bedding regularly to clean it and keep **fleas** away.

For many dogs, their crate is like a bedroom where they can go when they want to be alone or have some quiet time.

Kennels

If your dog will be spending a lot of time outside, you need to provide him with an outside shelter. A kennel will provide your dog with somewhere warm and dry to take shelter in when the weather is cold or wet, and somewhere shady to sleep in when it is sunny. Make sure the kennel you make or buy has a sloping, waterproof roof and solid sides so no drafts can get in. Remember that dogs can get lonely and bored by themselves, so do not leave your dog alone outside for long periods of time.

Bedtime

- Dogs like to sleep in the same place all the time. Keep their bed in the same spot and use the same blanket so it smells familiar, too.
- Dogs usually like to have their bed near where you and your family are.

Some people build their own kennel. You can download plans from the Internet or buy books with instructions.

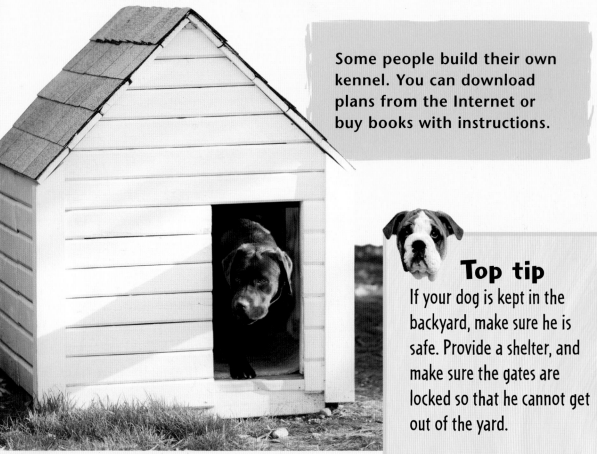

Top tip

If your dog is kept in the backyard, make sure he is safe. Provide a shelter, and make sure the gates are locked so that he cannot get out of the yard.

Collars

All dogs should have a collar to hold a **license** tag. Choose the correct collar for your dog's size and weight and make sure it fits properly. You should be able to slide two fingers between the collar and the dog's neck.

Some people use a **harness**, which fits around the chest instead of a collar. A harness is a good choice for a dog with a small head, or for dogs that wriggle out of their collars.

Leashes

You must have a leash for your dog. A dog on a leash is easier to control, especially in public places. Traffic is one of the biggest dangers to dogs, and using a leash near roads will keep your dog safe. You must choose the right leash for your dog's size and weight. Leashes come in different strengths for heavier and lighter dogs. You can also get leashes that you can shorten or lengthen as you are walking your dog.

A license tag usually has your dog's name and your phone number printed on it.

There are a wide range of leashes to choose from. Good pet shops will give you advice on the best leash for your dog.

Microchipping and tattooing

It is a good idea to ask your veterinarian to microchip or tattoo a special number on your dog. A microchip is a tiny computer chip injected under a dog's skin. A tattoo is usually put on a thigh or inside an ear. If your dog gets lost, people can look up the number on a special list and return the dog to you.

Train your dog to chew his chew toys and not things in your home!

Toys

Dogs need toys. Toys keep dogs from getting bored and can prevent some problem behaviors. For example, puppies chew a lot. They should learn that they can only chew on their toys, not furniture. Dogs also like to play with hard rubber balls, Frisbees®, and rings or knotted ropes. Make sure your dog toys are safe and do not have sharp edges, splinters, or small parts that your dog could swallow.

What are dog muzzles?

You only need a **muzzle** if your dog sometimes behaves badly. A muzzle fits over your dog's nose and mouth and stops him from biting people or other dogs or eating things he should not. Never muzzle your dog when it is very hot. He will not be able to pant and might overheat.

Get a leash strong enough to hold your dog, but lightweight enough to avoid straining or injuring him.

21

Taking Care of Your Dog

Your pet dog needs attention every day. This means giving her fresh water and food, but also keeping her clean, comfortable, and healthy.

Food and water

Some dog owners give their dogs canned food, but most choose dry food. It is easier to store and it helps keep dogs' teeth clean. You can soften dry food with water, or you can mix it with some canned food. Some people mix in a little cooked egg or vegetables to change the taste. Never give onions, because they are poisonous to dogs. Once opened, canned food should be stored in a refrigerator.

You should make sure your dog always has plenty of fresh water in her bowl. Remember that dogs drink more when they are hot or after exercising, just like you.

Feeding tips

- Read the labels on food packages or check with a veterinarian to get the right amount of food for your particular **breed** and age of dog.
- Feed your dog at the same time or times each day. Remove your dog's food bowl after ten to fifteen minutes so she gets used to the idea of eating at feeding times.
- Do not feed your dog bites of your own meals, or she will try to beg or steal food at your mealtimes.

Put your dog's food bowl in a quiet spot where she can eat without being disturbed.

Bones

Dogs love to chew raw bones, but do not give them cooked bones. Sharp pieces can break off and damage a dog's mouth. Never, ever give chicken bones, since they splinter and can get stuck in your dog's throat and stomach.

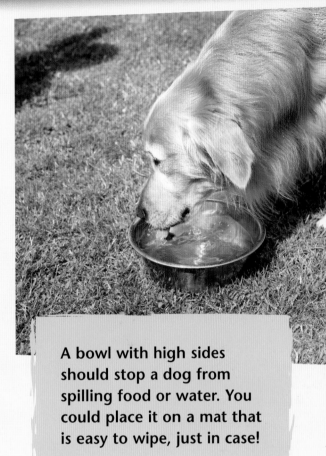

Bowls

Your dog needs her own bowls for food and water. Choose wide-bottomed, strong bowls that cannot be knocked over and are easy to clean. Many people choose steel or plastic bowls.

A bowl with high sides should stop a dog from spilling food or water. You could place it on a mat that is easy to wipe, just in case!

Dog treats

You can buy dog treats at pet stores, but dogs also enjoy treat foods such as crackers, cooked meat, or fresh vegetables. It is best not to give your dog sugary treats. Sugar will damage your dog's teeth and can make her fat and unhealthy. Chocolate contains a chemical that makes some dogs very sick.

Treats should be small and should not be given very often. This will keep them special for your dog.

Grooming

Dogs get dirt caught in their hair. This can make the hairs stick together, especially in long-haired dogs. It can also make the hair smell. Dogs lick themselves to stay clean, but you should brush your dog to help keep his hair clean and remove any loose, dead hairs that naturally fall out.

Most people brush their dog once or twice a week, using special dog combs and brushes. When you brush, look out for **fleas** and **ticks**.

If your dog's hair becomes so matted that it cannot be combed, you will need to have it cut. Ask an adult if he or she can do this, or contact a professional dog groomer.

Gently use a steel comb to remove tangles and loose pieces and a brush to smooth your dog's hair down.

Bathing

Most dogs only need to be bathed about once a month, unless they roll in something smelly. Ask an adult to help, and wear old clothes—bathtime can be messy! Bathe the dog in a bathtub or outside when the weather is warm enough. Comb or cut out any matted hair before washing the hair. Use dog shampoo, which you can get from a pet store. Make sure no soap gets in your dog's eyes. Then, rinse out all the soap and dry him with old towels.

Rinse out all the soap when bathing a dog, because dirt easily sticks to soap.

Your dog care schedule

Daily	Give your dog food and water. Wash out the food and water bowls with soapy water, rinse, and dry.
Weekly	Comb or brush your dog's hair. Clean his teeth.
Monthly	Wash soft bedding and toys. Check your dog's nails to see if they need clipping. Bathe your dog.
Yearly	Take your dog to the veterinarian for **vaccinations** and a checkup.

It can take some dogs a while to get used to teeth cleaning, so take it slowly.

Teeth and nails

Dogs can develop tooth and gum problems if their teeth are dirty. You or an adult can clean your dog's teeth. Use a paste made from baking soda and water, or you can buy dog toothpaste from veterinarians and pet store. Put the paste on a toothbrush or cloth wrapped around your finger. Carefully lift the dog's lips and rub the paste onto his teeth. Your dog will lick off the paste, leaving his teeth clean.

A dog's nails are usually kept short by running around and digging. If your dog's nails are getting too long, ask an expert or get a veterinarian to show you how to cut the nails properly.

Staying out of trouble

There are many dangers in people's homes that can cause trouble for dogs. For example, dogs can injure themselves by falling on stairs and slippery floors. They may get trapped under or inside furniture. Dogs chew or eat all sorts of items they find lying around. Some, such as medicine, can be harmful. Others, such as shoes, are expensive to replace if damaged. Dogs may escape and risk harm outside if you leave windows, doors, or backyard gates open.

When you first bring a puppy home, you need to train her to avoid household dangers.

Do not allow your dog to go into the bathroom. She might eat the dangerous cleaners and medicine stored there.

Some dog hazards

- Tape, tie, or hide electrical cords out of the way of your dog. She may get an electric shock if she chews the cables.
- Put houseplants, medicine, and household cleaners out of reach. These can cause serious sickness if chewed or swallowed.
- Pick up small items such as toys, coins, and batteries off the floor. These small items can choke a dog if swallowed.

Safe traveling

Many dogs enjoy traveling in a car with their owner, but some get carsick or frightened. Get your dog used to the car gradually. Begin by taking her on journeys to places she likes, such as favorite parks, rather than just visits to the veterinarian.

Dogs cannot wear seat belts, but you can make sure they stay safe if the car has to stop suddenly. They should travel in a crate or have a **harness** that clips to a seatbelt. Ask in a pet store to see what harnesses are available. There are many different products that should work in your car.

Warnings

- Never leave your dog alone in the car for long, and never on hot days. Cars can get so hot that dogs can get sick or even die inside.
- When you go on vacation, never leave your dog at home alone. Get someone to care for her as you normally would. You could ask a friend or a local boarding kennel.

When you are traveling with your dog, make sure she cannot jump up at the driver. This could cause an accident.

Training Your Dog

Training a dog can be hard work, but also really fun. It is essential to teach your dog some basic things, such as walking on a leash and coming when you call him. You may need to call your dog away from dangerous places, such as busy roads. A well-trained dog is also much easier to live with.

Tips for training dogs

- Make it fun. If you or your dog are not in the right mood, try another time.
- Keep training sessions to about five to ten minutes each time.
- Never punish a dog for getting it wrong. Just say "no" firmly and quietly.
- Do training after exercise so that the dog is calmer.
- Choose somewhere quiet to train, so that your dog will pay attention.

Training methods

The basic training technique is simple. When your dog does what you ask him to, reward and praise him. Say "good dog" and give him a pat and a tiny food treat. Remember, your dog may get it wrong many times before he learns, so be patient.

Dogs like to be petted and praised.

House-training a puppy

To **house-train** a puppy, first choose an area in the yard to be the dog's bathroom area. After your puppy has had food, had a nap, or when he looks around for somewhere to go, put him on a leash and take him outside to this area. If he goes to the bathroom, give him praise and a treat. If he does not, bring him inside again until you spot the signs that he wants to try again.

When dogs start to sniff around, they may be looking for a place to go to the bathroom.

Teach your puppy to wait through the night without going to the bathroom by putting him in a crate at bedtime. Dogs do not go to the bathroom where they sleep. You will have to get up a couple of times in the night. It will take a puppy about two weeks to learn this lesson.

If your puppy makes a mess indoors, put on gloves, remove the **urine** or **feces**, and flush them down the toilet. Clean the area with a cleaner that will remove the smell, called a deodorizing cleaner. If you do not get rid of the smell, your dog may continue to use the spot as a bathroom.

Warning

Never touch feces with bare hands because there is a risk of toxocariasis. This is a disease caused by the eggs of **roundworms**. Toxocariasis can make people blind. Always wear gloves or use a pooper scooper to deal with feces.

Lead your dog outside to his bathroom area when you think he wants to go.

Learning to sit

To teach your dog to sit, find a quiet place to train her. Start by holding a small treat by her nose. Move the treat up and back to encourage your dog toward a sitting position. As you do this, say "sit" clearly, just once. If she sits down, give her a pat, say "good dog," and give her a reward.

When your dog has learned to sit, take her to other places and get her to "sit" there, too. As your dog learns to sit, keep giving her lots of praise, but reduce the number of times you give a treat.

Reward your dog when she is good. This dog has learned to "sit."

Learning to stay

Once your dog has learned how to sit on command, try teaching her to stay as well. When she is sitting, hold back the treat and say "stay" once. If she stays, wait a few seconds and then give the treat. Repeat the lesson. Try to make it a little longer each time before you give the treat. Soon the dog will stay for a longer time. Then, try moving a little farther away when you tell your dog to stay. Soon she will learn to stay even if you go out of sight.

Other basic commands

You can teach many other commands using the same praise and reward technique. It is important to teach your dog to walk or run back to you when you call "come." This keeps your dog from running away or heading into unsafe areas, such as near traffic. You can also teach her to "heel," which means to walk closely beside you. It is also useful to teach your dog the command "leave it," so that she drops things that could harm her or that she should not bite.

Top tip

You can take your dog to training or obedience classes. Ask your veterinarian or check the library or Internet to find classes and times. Training classes are good for puppies because they meet other dogs and people in safe surroundings.

Get your dog used to hearing her name. Reward her if she comes when you call.

Exercise and Play

Dogs need exercise every day to keep them happy and healthy. Exercise and play help your dog sleep well, have more energy, and have good, strong bones and muscles.

Make sure your dog has his collar and **license** tag on before you go out for a walk.

Walking puppies

Puppies should not go outdoors until they have had all their **vaccinations**, at about twelve weeks old. At first, puppies may get scared when they meet new people, see new sights, or hear new sounds. Pick your puppy up and calm him down if he seems nervous, or take him home. Introduce him to new things slowly. For example, take him to quiet roads so he sees a few people and cars before going to a busy street.

Dogs stop and sniff a lot when they are out.

Dog fights

If your dog gets into a fight with another dog, never try to break up the fight by yourself. You may get badly bitten and scratched. Get adults to help.

Walk!

The amount of exercise a dog needs depends on his age, size, **breed**, and health. Check with your veterinarian if you are uncertain. In general, one long or two shorter walks each day will be fine, although larger dogs may need more. Never ride a bike, skateboard, or roller blade when holding your dog on a leash.

Running free

Most dogs like the chance to run free. They can only do this somewhere safe—for example, out in the country, on a beach, or in a fenced-in yard. Many cities have special dog parks that are fenced-in areas for dogs to play. Never let your dog run free near small children, farm animals, or traffic.

Walking tips

- Keep your dog under control at all times.
- Always clean up after him. Use a pooper scooper and put the waste in a bag and then in a trash can. Remember never to touch **feces** with your bare hands.
- Stop when your dog is tired.
- On hot days, give your dog water to drink and let him cool down in the shade.
- On cold days, do not stay out too long or he may get too cold.

Most dogs like the chance to run free and off the leash when they are somewhere safe.

Playtime

Dogs like all sorts of games. Most of them love playing tug-of-war with a toy or a rope. They will "fetch" and bring back a toy you throw for them. They like to catch Frisbees® or balls and play hide-and-seek. At home, keep your dog's toys in a box and out of reach so she does not get bored with them.

Dogs and puppies love playtime!

Controlling playtime

It is important that your dog does not get too excited during playtime. If this happens, she might hurt you, herself, or someone else. If she gets too excited, stop playing and put the toy away. If she jumps up, do not shout at her. Just turn away and ignore her until she behaves correctly. Then, when she sits down, pat and praise her.

Understanding your dog

It is good to understand what your dog means when she behaves in different ways. For example, when a dog's bark is high-pitched and her tail is wagging, she is excited and happy to see you. When a dog that has been playing walks away to lie down, it means she wants to rest.

Dog barks

Dogs have different barks to say different things, such as, "Someone is at the door." If you listen closely, you can learn what your dog's different barks mean.

When your dog wags her tail, it does not always mean that she is happy. It can mean she is uncertain. The position of the tail is a good clue. A stiff, straight-up tail means a dog is confident and ready to go. A tucked-down tail means a dog is nervous or **stressed**.

When your dog puts her front end down, her rear in the air, and barks at you, it means "Let's play!"

Many dogs are too big to lift. To pick up a small dog or puppy, put one hand under her chest. Use your other hand to support her back legs and rear end.

What to do if a dog bites you

Most dogs never bite, but your dog may accidentally bite you if she gets too excited. If this happens, tell an adult right away. If it is a minor wound, the adult can clean and treat it. See a doctor if the wound is deep.

Dog Health

When your dog is well, he looks healthy and has a lot of energy. You know your dog, so you will probably notice any changes in his health. If you are ever concerned about your dog's health, tell an adult so they can contact a veterinarian for advice.

A healthy dog has shiny hair, strong white teeth, pink gums, and a pink tongue.

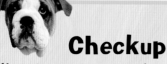

Checkup

Veterinarians are not just for emergencies. Soon after you get a new dog, take him to a veterinarian for a checkup. There are a lot of things to do in a checkup. For example, the veterinarian will look in the dog's ears and listen to his heart. Take your dog for a checkup each year to make sure he stays healthy.

You may find it difficult to hold your dog when the veterinarian examines him. Leave it to the veterinary nurse, who is experienced in doing this.

Vaccinations

All dogs must be **vaccinated** against some serious diseases, such as canine distemper, parvovirus, and rabies. Veterinarians give puppies a series of **injections** that help protect them from catching these diseases. They then give booster injections each year throughout the adult dog's life. It is important to keep a record of vaccinations to make sure your dog is protected. Your dog may need other vaccinations if he is going to another country with you or if he is going to stay in a boarding kennel.

Some possible signs of illness

- Eating less than usual: Your dog might eat less if the weather is hot, or when he gets older. Eating less can also be a sign of illness.
- Coughing or hacking: Your dog might cough a lot if he has a **virus** or has something caught in his throat.
- Red gums or eyelids: These may mean that your dog is **allergic** to something.
- Difficulty **urinating**: If your dog has trouble urinating, or if his **urine** is very dark, he may have a kidney problem.
- **Diarrhea** and **vomiting**: Dogs can get diarrhea or vomit if their food changes, or after eating something they should not. Diarrhea and vomiting can also be signs that your dog is seriously sick.
- Scratching or licking: Some scratching and licking is normal, but too much may mean your dog has a wound or irritating **parasites** such as **fleas**.
- Head shaking: There might be something wrong with your dog's ears.

Fleas and ticks

Fleas and **ticks** are common problems for dogs, especially when the weather is warm. Fleas and ticks are **parasites** that feed on blood from animals. They bite a dog's skin and make it itchy. They can also cause skin **infections** and **allergic** reactions. Fleas and ticks also bite people.

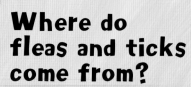

Where do fleas and ticks come from?

Fleas and ticks are found on plants, farm animals, other dogs, and wild animals. Fleas and their eggs also survive inside homes in carpets, curtains, under baseboards, and in unwashed pet bedding.

You should check your dog regularly for fleas and ticks when you **groom** her. They may get caught in the comb you use. You can easily get rid of them using treatments including powders, sprays, drops, and collars from a veterinarian or a pet store. Always wear gloves when you handle these treatments. Remember that any treatment only lasts for a few months. You will have to treat your dog regularly to make sure she does not have any more parasites.

If a dog has fleas, your home may have them, too. You can buy special treatments to kill fleas around the home.

Even the cleanest dogs pick up fleas.

Worms

It is common for dogs to have adult **roundworms** or hookworms living in their **intestines**. Dogs with worms may eat more than usual, look thinner, or continually clean or scratch their bottom. That is because adult worms tickle their bottoms as they lay eggs! Eggs in dog **feces** get onto the ground outside. Dogs accidentally eat worm eggs off the ground when they are out walking. You need to treat your dog for worms using pills or drops from a veterinarian or a pet store. You must repeat the treatment every few months to kill any new worms she gets.

Always ask an adult to help you when you handle medicine.

Heartworms

Adult heartworms look like spaghetti and live inside some dogs' hearts. They can make your dog very sick. Young heartworms live in dog blood. They spread from dog to dog when **mosquitoes** bite the dogs. That is why they are more of a problem in warmer, southern states, where more mosquitoes live. A veterinarian can tell if your dog has heartworms with a blood test and will give medicine to kill them.

Many people find that dogs take de-worming pills best when they are eating food.

39

Ear problems

If your dog's ears are looking very waxy, oozy, or puffy and smell bad, then he has an ear **infection**. When the ear is inflamed (red and sore), it is called canker. Mites, **bacteria**, and some types of yeast cause ear infections. Your veterinarian will be able to supply ear drops to get rid of ear infections. The veterinarian will also show you and your family how to safely clean your dog's ears.

Bites and wounds

Dogs can be bitten if they get into fights with other dogs or wild animals. They may also get wounds from sharp fences, prickly plants, or broken glass and sharp cans on the ground. Bites and wounds easily become infected with bacteria in the air and from the dog's saliva (spit) when he licks the wound.

It is important to clean any dirt out of a wound so that it heals.

Get an adult to carefully clean any wound with saltwater or **antiseptic** mixed with warm water. If the skin is badly torn, or the bite is deep, you should go to a veterinarian for treatment. This is because the wound will be difficult to clean and the infection may become more serious. The veterinarian will usually give an **antibiotic injection**, shave the hair around the wound to keep it clean, and stitch it up. Your dog should wear a plastic collar or "cone" to stop him from licking the wound or stitches, because this can slow down healing.

Top tip
Does your dog have very floppy ears or ears that are very hairy inside? Does he like to get into water? If the answer to these questions is yes, your dog will be more likely to get ear infections.

Broken bones

Dogs can break bones—if they fall from high places or are hit by cars, for example. If your dog is limping or his tail is an odd shape, he may have a broken bone. You need to take your dog to a veterinarian. He may need an operation to help mend the bone. He may also have to wear a plaster cast while the bone heals.

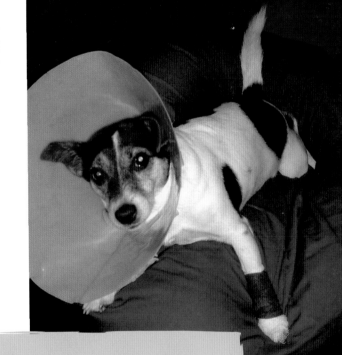

Warning
Be careful and patient. Your dog may get angry or unhappy because he is in pain from wounds, bites, or broken bones.

Your dog will not enjoy wearing a cone after his injury. However, the cone does not hurt, and it will help him get better.

Growing Old

Most dogs live long, happy, healthy lives, but as they get older, dogs slow down. Older dogs may not see or hear as well as they did, and they may get more illnesses. Being aware of these things can help you take better care of your elderly dog.

Exercise and diet

Older dogs have less energy, so they sleep more and play and walk less. Because they get less exercise, older dogs may gain weight. Being overweight is unhealthy, so ask your veterinarian about food mixes designed for older dogs. Older dogs often drink more water, too, so make sure your dog's water bowl is always full of fresh water.

Do all you can to make sure your elderly dog is comfortable.

Health checks

Older dogs are more likely to get health problems than younger dogs, such as a sore mouth and dry or clouded eyes. It is important to take your dog to a veterinarian for regular checkups. That way, a veterinarian should be able to spot and treat any health problems before they become serious.

You should also take your dog to the veterinarian if you spot any changes that concern you. For example, when you stroke your elderly dog, feel for skin lumps, which may be signs of **cancer**. Older dogs sometimes become incontinent. That means they cannot control when they pass **urine**.

The end of a life

Many dogs die peacefully in their sleep from old age. Sometimes a dog becomes so sick or old that your vet advises **euthanasia** to prevent her from suffering more. Euthanasia is when a veterinarian gives your dog an **injection** that painlessly stops her breathing. This is a difficult decision, but it may be the kindest thing.

Arthritis

Arthritis is a common problem in older dogs. This is where the joints become swollen and painful. Signs of arthritis are when a dog has difficulty standing up, climbing stairs, or jumping or if it is restless at night. Veterinarians can give medicines to help arthritis.

Losing a friend

Many people think of their pet dog as part of the family. It can be a terrible shock when your dog dies, and it is natural to be sad and upset. It can help to talk to someone about how you feel and about the happy times you had with your dog.

Burying your dog in a pet cemetery is a nice way to say goodbye and remember her.

Keeping a Record

You and your family will have many years to spend with your pet dog. In that time, lots of things will happen. For example, there may be special times you have spent with your dog on vacation. There will be times when she had to go to the veterinarian for treatment. It is easy to forget exactly what happened, so why not keep a record? Buy a big scrapbook and start to fill it up.

Things to put in your dog scrapbook

Here are some suggestions for your scrapbook:

- Your dog's history, such as where you got her and when, and information about her parents.
- A training record including, for example, the commands that your dog understands and how you usually praise her when she does something right.
- Eating preferences, such as the type of food she prefers, how much she eats, and her mealtimes.
- A medical diary including dates when your dog had **vaccinations**, de-worming pills, and **flea** treatments.
- Notes about her favorite games and places for walks.
- Photos of your dog with you, your family, with other pets, and in different moods. Try to take pictures in different places and from different angles, some close-up and some wide-angle.

Weight graph

See how your dog has grown by weighing her every month. Plot a line on graph paper with time on the x-axis (sideways axis) and your dog's weight on the y-axis (up-and-down axis). Make sure you choose a large enough piece of paper to fit all the data on!

Useful information

There is a lot of information about dogs you can collect for your scrapbook. Some will be general about dogs and some specific to particular **breeds**. You can read articles about dogs in newspapers, books, magazines, and on the Internet. You can watch TV programs and movies with dogs in them. You can contact **charities** that care for stray dogs. You can visit dog shows where many breeds are on display and dog experts are present to answer questions. Soon your scrapbook will be filling up.

Top tip

Your dog is a great subject for your own website or school project.

It can be really fun to take and choose photos of your dog.

Glossary

allergic when a person or animal reacts badly to something they eat, breathe, or touch

animal shelter place where abandoned or badly treated pets are cared for until they find a new home

antibiotic medicine that can cure some animal diseases

antiseptic chemical that can kill germs

bacteria tiny living thing. Some bacteria can cause diseases.

breeder someone who raises a particular type of animal to sell to people

breed kind of dog. Labradors and terriers are two different breeds of dog.

cancer serious disease that destroys the body's healthy cells

charity organization that raises money to help a cause

descendant member of a family who is born after others. You are a descendant of your parents, grandparents, and great-grandparents.

diarrhea runny feces (droppings)

domesticate to tame an animal so that it can live with people

euthanasia to give a sick or very old animal gas or an injection to stop its breathing. This is also called putting the animal to sleep.

feces waste that comes out of an animal's body; droppings

flea tiny living thing that lives on and irritates an animal's skin

groom to clean an animal's fur. Many animals groom themselves.

harness special kind of leash that goes around an animal's chest and legs

house-trained animal that is trained to go to the bathroom outdoors, not in the house

incisors long front teeth

infection illness that makes part of the body fill with pus

injection when a needle is used to put medicine into an animal's body

intestines part of the body that leads from the stomach to the anus

kennel club organization that keeps a register of pedigree, or purebred, dogs

license tag from the local government that lists a dog's owners, gives contact information, and proves that the dog has had the proper shots

litter number of baby animals born together

mammal animal that can feed its babies on milk from its own body

mosquito biting insect that can spread disease

muzzle covering for a dog's mouth to stop it from biting people

neutered when part of a male animal's body is removed so that he cannot make babies

parasite animal that lives and feeds on another animal's body

pedigree when a purebred animal has a list of its family

predator animal that catches other animals for food

roundworm parasite that lives in the stomachs of some animals

senses sight, smell, hearing, taste, and touch

spayed when part of a female animal's body is removed so that she cannot have babies

stressed feeling unhappy or nervous

suckle when a baby mammal drinks milk from its mother's body

tick parasite that lives on an animal's skin

urinate to produce urine (liquid waste)

urine liquid waste from the body

vaccination getting an injection that protects an animal against a disease

virus microscopic (tiny) living thing that can cause diseases

vomit to throw up

Further Reading

Coile, D. Caroline. *How Smart Is Your Dog?: 30 Fun Science Activities With Your Pet.* New York: Sterling, 2003.

Dennis-Bryan, Kim. *Puppy Care.* New York: DK, 2004.

Waters, Jo. *The Wild Side of Pet Dogs.* Chicago: Raintree, 2005.

You might also enjoy reading *Call of the Wild* by Jack London. This story is about a pet dog forced to become a sled dog in the harsh land of Alaska.

Useful Addresses

The following organizations work to protect animals from cruelty. They also help people learn how to care for their pets.

The American Society for the Prevention of Cruelty to Animals (ASPCA)
424 E. 92nd Street
New York, NY 10128
Tel: (212) 876-7700

The Humane Society of the United States (HSUS)
2100 L Street NW
Washington, D.C. 20037
Tel: (202) 452-1100

Internet

There are hundreds of pet websites on the Internet. The following sites give information about caring for animals, including dogs.

http://www.aspca.org
The website of the American Society for the Prevention of Cruelty to Animals (ASPCA). Under "Pet Care," check out "Dog Care."

http://www.hsus.org
The website of the Humane Society of the United States (HSUS).

You can also use the Internet to find out about dog clubs in your local area.

Disclaimer

All the Internet addresses (URLs) given in this book were valid at the time of going to press. However, due to the dynamic nature of the Internet, some addresses may have changed, or sites may have changed or ceased to exist since publication. While the author and publishers regret any inconvenience this may cause readers, no responsibility for any such changes can be accepted by either the author or the publishers.

Index